FINLAND

IN SEARCH OF ALVAR AALTO

Stephen and Scharlie Platt

www.leveretpublishing.com

Finland: In search of Alvar Aalto
First published - January 2026
Published by Leveret Publishing
56 Covent Garden, Cambridge, CB1 2HR, UK

Artek 60 Stool

ISBN 978-1-912460-34-2

FINLAND
In Search of Alvar Aalto

Alvar Aalto at his desk in studio at home Courtesy of © Alvar Aalto Foundation

Introduction

This journal is an account of a trip to give a paper at an Aesop Conference in Helsinki. (Aesop is an association of European schools of planning.) Helen Mulligan, an architect colleague from my company, Cambridge Architectural Research, was with us. She knew quite a bit about Finnish architecture and recommended we stay in the famous Torni Hotel. While in Helsinki, Scharlie and I were on a mission to see as much of Scandinavian design, particularly the works of Alvar Aalto. This account follows the walking routes we took around Helsinki.

Alvar Aalto (1898-1976)

Alvar Aalto was a revolutionary Finnish architect and designer recognised as a master of modern architecture. He was renowned for his human-centric approach, seamlessly integrating architecture, furniture, and nature in his designs. Aalto rejected the cold, strict geometry of his modernist contemporaries, instead favouring warm, natural materials, especially wood, flowing lines, and a sensitive use of light to emphasise the sensual aspects of design. He believed good design should be part of everyday life and created spaces that were comfortable for people. He designed everything from the building itself to the door handles, furniture, lighting, and textiles, ensuring a harmonious and complete environment. Growing up amid the Finnish landscape, Aalto incorporated natural forms and a dynamic relationship with the natural world in his work. Aalto worked closely with his first wife, Aino Aalto, an architect and designer in her own right, and later his second wife, Elissa, who helped complete many of his major projects.

It was typical for Aalto to design buildings as complete works of art with furniture and lighting. For example, the Beehive lamp, which is still in production, was originally designed for the Jyväskylä College of Education. Aalto's design work was marked by boldness, an element of surprise and a desire to experiment with different methods and materials. It was also characterised by the carefully considered relationship between the buildings and their surroundings.

But like other great artists, there was a darker side to his character, and Aalto was domineering and a philanderer. His two wives played a crucial part in the success of his practice. As well as being a qualified architect,

Alvar's first wife, Aino, was a trained carpenter, unlike Alvar. She designed many of the buildings' interiors and was created the pioneering bentwood furniture that made Aalto a famous name internationally. She was the chief designer and managing director of Artek, the company they founded in 1935 to manufacture their homewares, producing hundreds of textiles, lamps and glassware designs – many still on sale, and copied by countless other companies since.

It was Aino who went out to work every day, we are told, while Alvar stayed in his studio at home. "He had occasional coffee breaks, he hummed, then he went into his office to draw a line or two, and then he came back again," his daughter is reported as saying, looking at photographs of her father lounging on a daybed and sunbathing on the beach. Aino, meanwhile, was juggling work and children. "Alvar thought Aino's job was to take care of him first, and then came the children, and then her work."

The letters Aalto wrote while travelling hint at his philandering. "You need to commit a whole lot of sin before we're even," he writes. His nature was

Alvar Aalto in his home/office *Lehtikuva Oy—REX/Shutterstock.com*

charming and gregarious, and he excelled at networking, storytelling, and acting, which earned him a reputation as a speaker. As for his drinking, Aino pleads for "not so many cocktails as last time". Perhaps he learned this from an American architect, Frank Lloyd Wright. Aalto changed completely after meeting him. Gone was the casual Finnish country attire, replaced by double-breasted suits. His friendship with Laurance Rockefeller led to an exhibition at the Museum of Modern Art in New York in 1938, which catapulted the Aalto brand into the limelight. Aalto's Finnish pavilion at the New York World's Fair the following year was a sensation, making Aalto furniture the single most popular brand of modern furniture in the US until the end of the 1940s.

Following Aino's death from cancer in 1949, Aalto devoted himself completely to work and embarked on an energetic building spree. He won major competitions for the Helsinki University of Technology, the National Pensions Institute and Säynätsalo Town Hall – the last an enchanting building nestled in a forest.

His second wife, Elissa, was just as crucial to the office as Aino. But dominant Aalto tried to mould her into the image of Aino, even changing

Aino and Alvar Aalto *Courtesy of © Alvar Aalto Foundation*

her hairstyle and insisting that she wore only black and white clothes.

In the 1950s, he dabbled in standardised housing in Germany, bringing human-centred flexibility to the plans, allowing the system to be adapted to the specifics of each location. He abhorred the vulgar functionalism of so much prefabricated housing, introducing curves and irregular angles wherever possible. When someone asked him what module he used, he answered: "One millimetre." Visiting his buildings today, that meticulous devotion to detailed design, and the craftsmanship of natural materials, is a tonic compared with the crudeness of many contemporary buildings

Towards the end, he became increasingly introverted and bitter at what he saw as a lack of appreciation at home. As commissions dried up, he turned to alcohol more and more, and withdrew into the cocoon of his office. He drew up a grand plan for central Helsinki, but only one part of it, Finlandia Hall, was completed in 1971, five years before his death. It is hard to imagine his sense of rejection, given the years of attention his work has received ever since.

Elissa Aalto *Courtesy of © Alvar Aalto Foundation*

Preamble

Scandinavian design had a huge influence on my life. Before the war, my father, Norman Victor Platt, worked as a furniture buyer in Owen Owen's, a department store in Liverpool. Owen Owen came from a hill farm near Machynlleth. A severe depression forced the sale of the farm, and in 1868, Owen Owen opened a draper's shop in Liverpool which grew into a department store empire. Owen's daughter married into the Norman family, and in the 1930's, when my father worked there, the business was run by Duncan Norman. Owen Owen closed down in 1996.

Norman Victor Platt, my father, was born in 1900 and so escaped the First World War. Although he was older, he volunteered for the Second World War. Duncan Norman promised that his job would be there when he returned. Dad served in the North African Campaign with the 5th Royal Tank Regiment, part of the 7th Army (the Desert Rats). He was captured in the retreat from Tobruk in April 1941 after his tank was hit by an Axis tank and spent the rest of the war as a prisoner of war. When he returned home, he was suffering from post-traumatic stress and couldn't bear to meet people. And, unfortunately, Duncan Norman had promised my father's

Crusader Tank Tobruk North Africa April 1941

job to several successors to the post who had also gone to war and returned. So Dad began work as a commercial traveller working for jewellery trade manufacturers in Birmingham.

He believed in good taste, by which I believe he meant good design. He talked about G-Plan furniture; our own dining room suite of table, chairs, and sideboard was G-Plan by E. Gomme. The E. Gomme company was founded in High Wycombe in 1898 by Ebenezer Gomme, who at first made handmade chairs. In 1953, Donald Gomme, E Gomme's designer, produced a range of modern furniture, called G-Plan, that could be bought piece by piece to suit budgets. In the early 1960s, the government restricted hire purchase, and in response to competition from Danish furniture, the company introduced a Scandinavian range, designed by Ib Kofod-Larsen. From an early age, I was indirectly exposed to Scandinavian design.

Terence Conran began his design practice in 1956 with the Summa furniture range, and in 1964 he opened the first Habitat shop in Chelsea, focusing on contemporary design for housewares and furniture. This store, with its quarry-tiled floor, whitewashed brick walls, white-painted slatted ceilings and spotlights, created a sense of space and became the template

Habitat shop Tottenham Court Road, opened 1966

for further stores. Habitat grew into a large chain, the first retailer to bring such designs to a mass audience. I got married in 1965, and Habitat was a revelation. On a student grant, their products were out of my price range, but they inspired me to make my own furniture.

"The Stanley book of Designs for making your own furniture" was published in 1966. It was original in several ways. It featured nine designs by nine different designers. There were photographs and biographies of each designer, which were interesting. But more importantly, there were attractive colour photographs, along with exploded axonometric drawings and cutting lists. The main materials used were solid beech, birch ply, and teak-veneered chipboard. Although I never slavishly followed any of the designs, over the next ten years, I made similar versions of the workshop bench, bookcases, beds, dining table, three-piece suite, and kitchen cabinets. I stopped using chipboard, but I have used a lot of birch ply, beech, and reclaimed pitch pine. The things I appreciated about good design were clarity and utility. I found the consistent and coherent use of materials and shapes aesthetically pleasing. I also found I liked the feel and look of wood.

In the early 20th century, the Industrial Revolution and Germany's

Stanley Book "designs for making your own furniture"

Bauhaus school inspired European designers to create furnishings free of ornamentation, yielding streamlined, machine-inspired functionalism. Scandinavian designers put their own spin on the style, incorporating elements of their longstanding craftsmanship traditions, particularly light-colored woods. Nordic countries are known for clean-lined, functional, and naturally formed design, bringing modernism to the masses by making it more humanistic.

Terence Conran and Habitat were significantly influenced by Scandinavian design, especially Finnish Modernism, adopting Alvar Aalto's human-centric approach, natural materials, organic forms, functionalism, and integration of nature, providing an alternative to stark modernism. Aalto's focus on human needs, comfort, and the feeling of a space resonated with Conran's democratic design ethos. Aalto's pioneering use of bent plywood and native light woods became iconic, emphasising light, warmth and connection to nature, a core tenet of Finnish design. The fluid, undulating lines of Aalto's Savoy vase and furniture, inspired by Finnish landscapes, introduced soft, natural shapes into modern design. Aalto didn't just design buildings; the Aalto studio also designed the furniture, fittings and lighting. He viewed

Aalto chair and stools in Savoy Cafe, Halsinki

furniture and objects as complete works of art, functional yet beautiful, which aligned with Habitat's goal of well-designed everyday items.

Conran translated this design philosophy into mass-produced, high-quality, affordable furniture and home goods for Habitat, democratising good design. Habitat's aesthetic embraced Scandinavian principles of simple, clutter-free design, natural textures, and functional lighting, creating liveable, welcoming spaces. Habitat's products, much like Aalto's philosophy, incorporated natural wood, plants, and organic shapes, bringing the outdoors in. Conran and Habitat took the core Scandinavian principles of warmth, nature, human scale, and functional beauty, championed by Aalto, and made them accessible to a broader public, thereby defining a generation's approach to modern living.

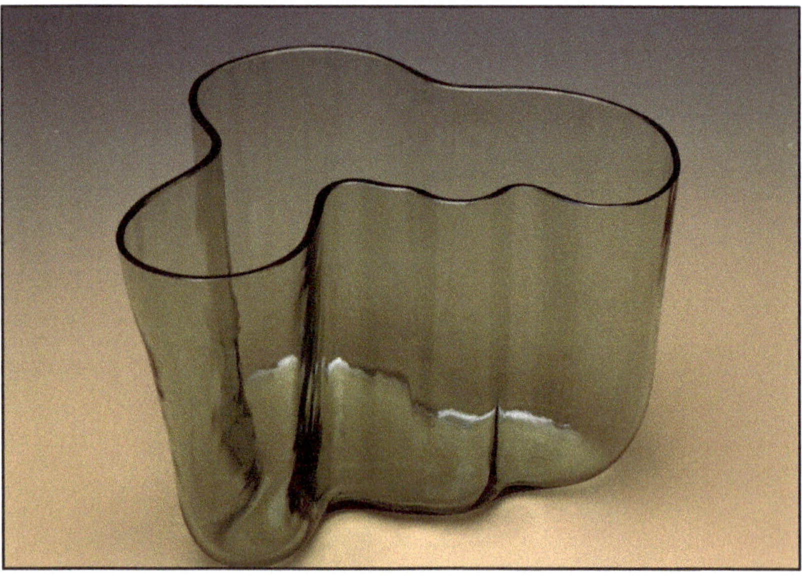

Aalto 'Savoy' Vase, courtesy of Aalto Foundation

Monday 5 July

We had a calm flight from Manchester to Helsinki yesterday. Looking down on England's green fields in the golden afternoon sun. Passing over Newcastle, we sailed above the clouds and looked down on puffy cotton wool until we reached the coast of Sweden. Then thousands of small islands dotted like a tortoiseshell, and Finland itself, endless forests and lakes and a smooth descent to Helsinki.

The city bus was waiting outside the airport, and we stowed our cases and set off at once. The bus took us to the central railway station, a ten-minute walk from our hotel. It was after 10 pm, and the receptionist said they had stopped serving and that we would find food at the Olive restaurant if we got there before 11 o'clock, when their kitchen closed.

It was bright daylight. It doesn't really get dark at this time of the year. We dropped our luggage in our superior bedroom, which Steve had managed to get a reduction on, and made our way to the Olive restaurant. The food was welcome, but expensive and of poor quality – limp lettuce and croutons for the Caesar salad, burnt ravioli and glasses of mediocre red wine. It was good to get into bed under silky white duvets, with a choice of

Hotel Tomi

three pillows each. Pillows seem to be a big thing here. The bedroom, like the hotel, conforms to the Scani aesthetic of plain, clean lines with a white ceiling and distinctive moulded alcoves. A frieze of leaves and acorns separates the ceiling from the pale green walls. The floor-to-ceiling white muslin curtains pleasantly filter the bright light.

Hotel Torni

The Hotel Torni is a historic, four-star hotel centrally located in Kamppi, the so-called Helsinki Design District. It's known for its Art Deco and Art Nouveau rooms, a rooftop bar with panoramic views, and excellent restaurants. The hotel was designed by Finnish architects Bertel Jung & Valter Jung in 1928, and has 14 stories. When it opened in 1931, it was the tallest building in Finland, a position it maintained until 1976. The interior of the building was completely renovated in 2005. Scharlie loved the ancient, exposed-ironwork elevator. The elevator was supplied by the Finnish elevator company Kone, founded in Helsinki in 1910.

Artists frequented Torni's restaurants, leaving behind plenty of visual art and fragments of world literature. Art collection at Torni continue to this

Lift in Tomi Hotel

Ateljee Bar, Torni Hotel

Restaurant, Hotel Torni

day and unique works can be found throughout the building.

During the hotel's construction, an access structure was erected on the roof intended to allow docking for the airship Graf Zeppelin, which visited Helsinki in September 1930. The idea was that the airship could dock on the roof of Torni, and passengers would descend by ladder to the bar for a cocktail. The mooring never happened, but the access remains visible in the ceiling of the Ateljee Bar.

The Jugendstil residential building Kyllikki, located next to Torni, was integrated into the hotel in 1981. This addition provided 50 rooms in the national romantic style. The furniture and decor of the magnificent Kyllikki suites were designed by Eliel Saarinen. We stayed in one of these Jugendstil suites.

The green copper spire rising above the trees is Hotel Torni, a classic Helsinki landmark.

Our Jugenstil room in Torni Hotel

Tuesday 6 July

We just made it to the dining room before it closed and had an elegant and leisurely breakfast. What a contrast to the frenzy of the last few days. We also made the most of the abundant offerings to craft a satisfying lunch, which we smuggled out in napkins. Over breakfast, Steve teased out a sightseeing route from the guidebook for us to walk. He has been very patient with my slow pace because of my painful foot. I couldn't walk without my flip-flops. They don't fit my image of myself, and I must look like a right old lady ambling along in my comfortable trousers, loose white shirt, and white cotton sun hat. Age comes on so gradually that you get used to it, and then you become aware that you are moving in ways you remember your grandparents using. When my foot is better, I will lose more weight and spring back into a life of vigorous movement.

Helsinki Railway Station

We started at the railway station – monolithic statues guarding the entrance and majestic inside. The station, designed by Eliel Saarinen and completed 1919, blends National Romanticism with early Nordic modernism, creating a

Central Station Helsinki designed by Eliel Saarinen 1919

station that is symbolic, functional, and memorable. Most iconic are the four "Lantern Bearers", granite figures holding glowing globes. Inside, the main hall is tall and clear and designed to handle crowds without chaos. Unlike many European stations, it avoids baroque drama. Instead, it offers clarity and calm, and a meeting point under the clock.

Scharlie fell into conversation with a man sitting on a bench, who asked what she was photographing. They commiserated with each other about the World Cup defeats of England and Ghana – all the referee's fault, of course. He is here studying for a PhD in health administration and says he intends to return to Ghana to enter politics, but he must save money first. An older lady came up and sat next to him. She added that you need cash and good character to succeed in Ghanaian politics. The young man said Ghana was now a true democracy. Their president had made a speech saying that, in the World Cup qualifier, Ghana's top goal scorer should not be blamed for missing his penalty kick. He had intended to succeed, which was what mattered. We would have loved to continue the conversation. It would have been interesting to learn about Finland from the perspective of a Ghanaian who had lived here for more than eight years. After we left, I

Cafe, Central Station

regretted not having found a way to extend our acquaintance. Perhaps we will bump into them again. He recommended a Finnish restaurant – proper traditional food, although he said they usually ate African food.

Sanomatalo

The area is full of new lavish high-tech buildings and high-rise flats. Steve commented that they work because they are set in large, well-planted, well-maintained civic spaces. Sanomatalo is an office building in central Helsinki, near the station, and is one of the most modern. It was designed by Jan Söderlund and Antti-Matti Siikala and completed in 1999. It was the first all-glass building in Helsinki, and environmentalists protested the glass walls, fearing they might cause bird strikes.

Eduskuntatalo — the Finnish Parliament House

In contrast, the parliament building has a Neoclassical facade, designed by J. S. Sirén and completed in 1931. Built from Finnish granite, which is heavy, tactile, and weathering well. It conveys endurance and rootedness in the landscape. There are no gates or fences, symbolising accessibility and democracy.

Eduskuntatalo — the Finnish Parliament House

Sanomatalo office building

Finlandia Hall

The Finlandia Hall is a congress and event venue in the centre of Helsinki, overlooking Töölönlahti Bay. The building was designed by Aalto in 1962 and was completed in 1971. Every detail was designed by Aalto. Each lamp, piece of furniture, panel, flooring, door handle, and decorative wallboard is a reflection of Aalto's language of natural forms. The hall was the only part of a development plan around Töölö Bay. Its main feature is a tower-like section with a sloping roof. Alvar Aalto's design principle was that a high, open space would improve acoustics. A lattice ceiling hides the space from the audience, but creates the deep post-echo of church towers. Aalto used Italian Carrara marble on both indoor and outdoor surfaces to contrast with black granite. For Aalto, the marble was a tie to the Mediterranean culture, which he wanted to bring to Finland.

Temppeliaukio Church

The treat of the day was the rock church, hewn from granite, with a circular glass-and-copper dome. Temppeliaukio is a Lutheran church in the Töölö neighbourhood, designed by Timo and Tuomo Suomalainen and

Finlandia Hall

Temppeliaukio (Rock) Church

Altar

opened in 1969. The interior was excavated and built directly out of solid rock and is bathed in natural light, which enters through the skylight surrounding the centre copper dome. The dome is lined with 22 kilometres of copper and supported on the rock walls by reinforced concrete beams. The interior walls are of rugged rock and rubble, and an ice-age crevice serves as the altarpiece.

The church is frequently used as a concert venue because of its excellent acoustics, shaped by the rough, virtually unworked rock surfaces. The iconic rock walls were not included in the original competition entry. But when conductor Paavo Berglund shared his knowledge of acoustics from some of the best music halls, and the acoustical engineer Mauri Parjo set the requirements for the wall surfaces, the Suomalainen brothers discovered they could meet all the acoustical requirements by leaving the rock walls exposed in the Church Hall.

Inside, a sign read, "Please do not talk." We went in and sat across from a Steinway piano. After a few minutes, a young Japanese man sat down at the piano and began to play a varied programme of styles and composers, all from memory. People came and went, lighting candles and taking photos.

Afternoon piano recital

Eventually, we ambled over to within a few yards of the piano, where we could watch his hands moving and imagine the sensation of touching the keys. The pleasure and sensory nature of the experience gave Scharlie goose pimples. Afterwards, he said he played every day from 10 am to 2 pm in July. We went on to see the Sibelius Monument in the Sibelius Park and the contrasting styles that defined Helsinki housing – traditional detached timber houses and multi-story modern apartments.

Villa Taivallahti

The Villa Taivallahti is a well-known historic wooden house just west of Sibelius Park, with yellow-painted timber walls and a white decorative trim. It was built in the 1890s, originally a private seaside villa. Today it functions as a restaurant and event venue and is advertised as a luxury lakeside holiday home with private beach access, a sauna, a fireplace, and a terrace.

Kesäkatu 6,

Kesäkatu is a housing complex in Taka-Töölö, comprising three curving blocks of flats from the late 1990s, designed by Timo Vormala of Gullichsen

Kesäkatu apartment block

Vormala Architects. It has large glazed balconies/terraces and a park-like inner courtyard.

Sibelius Park

Sibelius Park is a beautiful, small park nestled in the heart of Hämeenlinna. The park is named after the famous Finnish composer, Jean Sibelius, who was born nearby. The centrepiece of the park is a large statue of young Jean Sibelius. But we had come to see the Sibelius Monument

The Sibelius Monument is like a silver pipe organ set in an amphitheatre of pine trees. You can walk underneath it and tap the pipes to release different notes. It was designed in 1967 by Ella Hiltunen, a Finnish sculptor, and commissioned by the Sibelius Society after the composer's death in 1957. It's worn well. Apparently, when the wind blows, it makes music, but today there is no wind.

From an early age, Sibelius showed a strong interest in nature, often wandering the countryside when the family moved to Loviisa on the coast for the summer months. For most of his life, Sibelius lived in the countryside at Ainola, his timber home built near Lake Tuusula in Järvenpää

Sibelius Monument

Ainola, Sibelius' home

Sibelius' wife, Aino, and children family in Ainola

in 1904. Although the roof is tile and has a steeper pitch, Ainola is a chalet style house similar to our home, Leveret Croft.

Sibelius' wife Aino, had the same name as Aalto's first wife. Sibelius was famous for his excessive wining and dining in Helsinki, spending exorbitant amounts on champagne and lobster. His lifestyle had a disastrous effect on Aino, who was driven to retire to a sanatorium, suffering from exhaustion.

We made our way back through Central Park beside a lake – noisy seagulls overhead and one small speckled juvenile looking lost in a car park. They seem to be carving up the end of the park near our hotel with vast new buildings, which is a pity. We walked east towards the Olympic Stadium. This area of 6-storey apartment blocks around a shared courtyard is typical of much of Helsinki. This is the perimeter plan form of urban development advocated by architects and urban theorists Sir Leslie Martin and Lionel March at the Martin Centre, where I was in the early seventies. They used quantitative analysis to demonstrate that the courtyard form offers more useful open space and better light than high-rise towers. Humalistonkatu 8, built in the 1930s with white/cream render and steel-railed balconies, is one of these functional housing blocks east of Sibelius Park.

Olympic stadium

The stadium was built for the 1952 Summer Olympics and designed by Yrjö Lindegren and Toivo Jäntti. It's an icon of the functionalist style of architecture. Construction began in 1934 and was completed in 1938, with the aim of hosting the 1940 Summer Olympics, which were cancelled due to World War II. The tower is a striking landmark, rising 73 metres.

Since March 2007, a Eurasian eagle-owl has been living in the stadium. Due to strict conservation laws, no physical attempt to persuade the bird to leave has been allowed. In 2007, during a Euro qualifying match, the owl delayed play by ten minutes after perching on a goalpost. The Belgians unexpectedly lost the match, claiming the owl had "disturbed their rhythm of playing". This elevated the owl to national hero status. The owl was later christened Bubi and named Helsinki's Resident of the Year.

Olympic Stadium, designed by Yrjö Lindegren and Toivo Jäntti. 1952

Wednesday 7 July

Cafe Aalto

Today we began our Alvar Aalto trail properly, and we met Helen for coffee at one of Helsinki's best cafes, the famous Aalto Cafe. Café Aalto is on the second floor of the Academic Bookstore building in central Helsinki. Aalto designed the bookstore building, the Kirjatalo, the 'Book House', and its original interior in 1955. When office rents rose in Helsinki in the mid-1980s, the cafe was forced to close. However, the furniture was saved. Elissa Aalto, Alvar Aalto's second wife, granted permission for the café to use the Aalto name. Café Aalto was established in its current location within the Academic Bookstore in 1986 and has been a family business ever since. From here we walked east towards the central square and harbour.

Cafe Aalto with Helen

Cafe Aalto and Scharlie

Akateeminen Kirjakauppa, Academic Bookstore, desined by Aalto 1955

Kapelli

The Kappeli Café has one of the richest traditions of any meeting-place in Helsinki, and the legendary terrace is a popular place in summer. It opened in 1867 and became a local favourite among poets, writers, and artists in the late 19th and early 20th centuries. It began with a pastry-and-lemonade kiosk built by confectioner Johan Daniel Jerngren in 1840. The kiosk resembled a chapel and was thus known as Kappeli. In 1916, the restaurant Kappeli became a summer-only venue. The restaurateur Lundbom renovated the pavilion and kitchen, and the restaurant became known for its good food. However, over the years, the building deteriorated because of humidity and cold weather. In 1976, the restaurant was renovated for year-round use, and in the 1980s, Kappeli was one of the few restaurants in Helsinki that stayed open until four in the morning. The music in the Esplanade Park and the bustling Market Square, create a unique atmosphere. The café offers a daily soup lunch, along with sweet and savoury delights.

Kapelli Restaurant

Virgin Oil Co. Building

The Virgin Oil Co. Building at Mannerheimintie 5 is unique. Formerly a restaurant and club, it was known for its distinctive, controversial Art Nouveau (Jugendstil) style, which contrasted with its neoclassical neighbours. The building features a strikingly ornate facade, often highlighted by the restaurant's prominent orange-and-red signage, and was once considered an eyesore but is now a noted architectural landmark.

Central Market

The Kauppatori, 'Market Square', is a bustling open-air hub by the harbour, selling fresh produce, souvenirs, and street food such as salmon soup and reindeer sausage. It's vibrant in summer, with seasonal markets and events like the October Herring Market. Until the early 19th century, the site was the muddy bottom of Kaupunginlahti Bay and was used as a marketplace by local fishermen, who moored their boats at the piers and sold fish.

Filling the bay required a great deal of rubble to create a wide market square and three harbours: one at the east end for ships bound for Sveaborg, one at the western end for fishing boats, and one to the south

Virgin Oil Co. Building, designed by Armas Lindgren and Wivi Lönn. 1910

for steamships. We then crossed the canal separating Katajanokka from the mainland, which was dug during the construction in the early 1830s.

Central Market

Kauppatori, Market Square

Uspenski Cathedral

Uspenski Cathedral is the main cathedral of the Orthodox Church of Finland. It was designed by the Russian architect Aleksey Gornostayev and completed after his death in 1868 by Ivan Varnek. In the construction of the cathedral, 700,000 bricks were brought over in barges from the Bomarsund Fortress that had been demolished in the Crimean War. The cathedral has several valuable icons, two of which have been stolen. The icon of St. Nicolas, the Wonder Worker, was stolen in 2007 in broad daylight while hundreds of tourists were visiting the cathedral. Another icon, the Theotokos of Kozeltshan, was stolen in June 2010, but it was later recovered when one of the robbers, jailed for the theft, had a change of heart and revealed its location. It had spent 8 months in the ground but remained nearly immaculate.

From here, we passed a somewhat eccentric apartment block with a skybridge at Kiinteistö Oy Mastokoukku. It was designed by Jyrki Tasa of Arkkitehdit NRT Oy and constructed in 2006.

Uspenski Cathedral

Kiinteistö Oy Mastokoukku, designed by Jyrki Tasa 2006.

Jugendstil, Katajanokka

Our return took us through an area of Jugendstil, 'Youth Style', buildings, the German and Scandinavian version of Art Nouveau, built 1890-1910, and characterised by flowing organic lines, floral motifs, and the aim of modernising design by rejecting historic styles in architecture, decorative arts, and graphics. It merged natural forms with geometric elements, focusing on harmony between art and everyday life. In Helsinki, there are over 600 Jugend buildings; more than in Barcelona.

Dolphin Fountain, Market Square

The iconic Havis Amanda statue and fountain were designed by Ville Vallgren and installed in the Market Square in 1908. It features a bronze nude sea maiden rising from the water, spouting from four dolphins, and surrounded by seals, symbolising Helsinki's rebirth, and is a popular landmark and a traditional meeting place on May Day.

Jugenstil apartments, Katajanokka

Thursday 8 July

Rautatalo, the Helsinki Energy Office Building

The Rautatalo was designed by Alvar Aalto and completed in 1955. It was commissioned for the Finnish Hardware Association, after which it is named: Rautatalo translates as 'Iron House'. The exterior of the building is dark and austere, clad with copper plate on its main façade and brown brick on the side elevation. Aalto designed it to complement the height and proportions of the adjacent earlier building, created in classical style by Eliel Saarinen. In contrast to the exterior, the interior is light and airy, making extensive use of white Carrara marble and travertine. At the heart of the interior space is an enclosed atrium, known as Marmoripiha, 'Marble Garden', naturally lit through 40 skylights, its design inspired by Mediterranean architecture. The atrium was the highlight of the original architecture, bringing the business and office spaces together, and for many years, the original 'Iron House Café', which operated in the Rautatalo Marmoripiha, was an important part of Helsinki's social life.

Rautatalo

Marmoripiha, 'Marble Garden, Rautatalo, designed by Aallto 1955

Restaurant in Marmoripiha,, Rautatalo, designed by Aallto 1955

Door handle , Rautatalo

Fountain, Rautatalo

Savoy Restaurant

The nearby Savoy Restaurant is an equally famous social space. It is located in a building designed by Aino and Alvar Aalto in 1937, and furnished by Artek, which they had founded two years earlier. It is noted for its use of rich woods, functional elegance, and iconic designs like the Savoy vase, furniture and lighting. It was renovated in 2019 by Studio Ilse, and the original functionalist interior, of plywood and exposed brick, was preserved.

Although they weren't open, the maître d' kindly allowed us to look around and take photos. The restaurant is long and narrow, resembling a tram or a ship's saloon and seemed a lovely, intimate space for dining. The windows overlook the Esplanadi Park. At the time of its opening in 1937, Savoy had an air conditioning device keeping the hall clean of cigar smoke, which was unusual at the time. The most famous of its clients was Field Marshal Carl Gustaf Emil Mannerheim, and the Savoy is widely regarded as a hallmark of Finnish cuisine. (Mannerheim led the Whites in the Finnish Civil War of 1918, was the commander-in-chief of the Finnish Defence Forces during World War II, and the president of Finland 1944–1946).

There was a cloudburst and rainstorm on the way back.

Savoy Restaurant designed by Aino and Alvar Aalto 1937

Savoy Restaurant

Grand piano, Savoy Restaurant

Savoy Restaurant in 2010

Cloud burst

Friday 9 July

Puu-Vallila

Today we went on a tour of Old Vallila, an area of wooden houses, with a group from the conference, including Bahar and Isin, my PhD students from Nottingham University. Entering Old Valllila you get the impression you have left the city behind and are in a small old village.

Housing was an urgent social issue in Helsinki at the turn of the 20th century, and, in 1907, the city appointed a committee to investigate measures to increase the supply of affordable dwellings. The result of the committee's work was Puu-Vallila, Helsinki's Wooden House District, the first systematically planned worker housing area in the city, designed as a 'garden city'. The city architect Karl Hård af Segerstad drew a plan for Vallila, that was inspired by the vernacular architecture in Sweden and Germany and was streamlined by standardising the fixed parts of the building. Despite the standardisation, the two-storey houses were individually designed, and the painted weatherboarding gives each a consistent but distinct appearance. The houses have high gambrel roofs, which the building

Puu-Vallila, wooden house district 1910-13

code allowed for residential use. Façades have cross-gables and window bays. The structural frames are made of jointed, sawn logs, and the walls are clad with timber boards. The design is simple, yet the houses retain the style and elegance of villa architecture. The architects involved in the project were Armas Lindgren (Finnish architect who worked with Eeliel Saarinen and taught Alvar Aalto), Jussi Paatela (Finnish architect who has designed many hospitals across Finland), his brother Toivo Paatela, and Karl Hård af Segerstad (the Helsinki City Architect from 1907 until 1921). The land was divided into plots in 1908, and the first phase of construction was completed between 1910 and 1913.

Old Vallila was a disappointment for the city. Although it was intended to provide ideal housing, most working-class families continued to live in cramped one-room flats. Over time, appreciation for the area waned, and plans were proposed to redevelop it. In the 1970s, the residents rose up to defend their district. Old Vallila was protected in the town plan in 1980, and renovations began. The renovation project was awarded a Europa Nostra honorary mention in 1990. The lush gardens and subtle retrofitting have made the district an attractive oasis in the middle of the stone town.

Garden in Puu-Vallila

Puu-Vallila

Puu-Vallila

The rest of the Vallila neighbourhood, like much of Helsinki, is dominated by tall apartment buildings, most of which date back to the 1920s and 1930s, and the small wooden houses are well hidden behind their tall neighbours. These apartment blocks were also intended to provide working-class living conditions and to foster safe, strong communities. I know which of the two I'd prefer to live in. I was obviously enamoured of the wooden houses since Leveret Croft, my own home, built in 1904, is timber. There is nothing that compares to a wooden house. A unique relationship has evolved between humans and trees, wood being one of the most versatile organic materials that has been present in our daily lives since the beginning of civilisation.

The houses are surrounded by nature and greenery. Most have sheltered gardens and internal courtyards. In places, the bedrock granite outcrops are exposed as mini-parks. Although it was not the intention to design Puu-Vallila as a garden city, its design follows similar principles to those used to design Puu-Käpylä, another wooden district in Helsinki, which was designed as a garden city. Seeing these houses are still inhabited and well-maintained, and seeing the gardens filled with tables, chairs, flower pots, and children's toys it seems Old Vallila is a good place to live.

Puu-Vallila, detached villa

Vallila Library

They were renovating the internal courtyard of the Vallila Library and we were able to take photographs. Vallila Library, built in 1991, was described by its architect, Juha Leiviskä, as the first building where he succeeded in embodying his ideas of architectural form. The library and its neighbouring kindergarten are situated on a small plot within Puu-Vallila. In the original plans, the library was proposed in a more central location along the main street and the present site on the periphery was not the architect's first choice.

The library is timber frame. Some of the detailing is reminiscent of designs I used in constructing pergolas for clients of Scharlie's Garden Design. The focal point of the library's interior is what the architect calls 'the piazza', the building's highest space. The building was refurbished in 2008.

Vallila Library, designed by Juha Leiviskä, 1991

Renovation of Vallila Library inner courtyard 2010

Dipolo Conference Centre Aalto University, designed by Raili and Reima Pietilä

Dipolo Conference Centre

From here, we went to the Dipolo Conference Centre on the Otaniemi campus of Aalto University. Otaniemi is one of the most interesting sites of Finnish architecture. Designed by Raili and Reima Pietilä in 1966. The general plan of the campus was realised by Alvar Aalto, and his office oversaw the main building, the Otahalli sports hall, built for the Olympics, and several other buildings. The older dormitories, the Servin Mökki restaurant and the Otaniemi chapel were designed by Heikki and Kaija Siren.

By now, I was used to taking the metro from near our hotel and walking along the tree-lined boulevards to the conference venue. Designed by Raili and Reima Pietilä, Dipolo was completed in 1966 and is widely regarded as an architectural gem. The design blends into the surrounding natural bedrock and forest, featuring a sculptural copper-and-granite facade. Originally built as a student residence, Dipoli has served as a conference centre for decades and now houses Aalto University's main building.

Main Auditorium of Dipolo Conference Centre

Aalto University Undergraduate Centre designed by Alvar Aalto 1965

Aalto-yliopiston kirjast building, designed by Alvar Aalto 1965

Saturday 10 July

Aalto House and Studio

Today we caught a bus to visit Alvar Aalto's home. The bus driver was very proud of Aalto's renown and spoke of his impact on Finnish culture. We were excited by the prospect. The front entrance is plain and somewhat austere. The house's severe streetside elevation is intentional, but softened by climbing plants and a slate path. Once inside the house, however, all is delightfully spacious, light and comfortable, and one could imagine it would be pleasant living and working here. The Aalto House is a cosy, intimate building for living and working, designed by two architects for themselves, using simple, uncluttered materials. In contrast to Villa Mairea, another house the couple designed, this house is not a luxurious residence but a cosy, intimate living space.

In 1934, Aino and Alvar Aalto acquired the site in the almost unspoiled Munkkiniemi district and started designing their own house, which was completed in 1936. Aalto became acquainted with Munkkiniemi and developed a liking for it while working on design along the shores of

Aalton House, front entrance, designed by Aino and Alvar Aalton 1936

Laajalahti Bay. The proposition never materialised, which was perhaps just as well because it would have meant that the shore would have been lined with long, white apartment buildings.

The house was designed as both a family home and an office, and these two functions are clearly visible from the outside. The slender mass of the office wing is built in white-painted, lightly rendered brickwork. The cladding material of the residential side is dark-stained timber battens. The building has a flat roof and a large south-facing terrace.

There are already signs of the 'new' Aalto in the Aalto House, of the Romantic Functionalist. The plentiful use of wood as a finishing material and four open hearts built in brick also point to this.

Aalto lived in the house until his death in 1976, and after that, his second wife, Elissa Aalto, lived there until her death in 1994. The house was protected by a law in 1982, and it was renovated inside and out in the early years of the new millennium, funded by the Finnish Ministry of Education and Culture and the City of Helsinki.

Aalto House, rear view

Aalto House living room

Aalto House living room

Aalto House office/studio

Aalto House office/studio

Drinks trolley

Single bedroom, Aalto House

Sunday 11 July

Tallinn, Estonia

Today we signed up for a day trip to Tallinn, the capital of Estonia. Our guide collected us from our hotel at 9 and drove us to the ferry, which took just two hours to cross the Gulf of Finland. Until the first half of the 20th century, Tallinn was known as Reval. It was annexed to the USSR in the summer of 1940, and after the German retreat in September 1944, the city was reoccupied by the Soviet Union. Tallinn once again became the capital of a de facto independent country on 20 August 1991. Today, Tallinn has the highest number of startup companies (per capita) in Europe and is the birthplace of many international high-tech companies, including Skype.

We had come to see the Old Town, one of Europe's most walkable historic districts. The medieval street layout creates a pedestrian paradise with numerous car-free zones. It is a World Heritage Site spanning just 113 hectares, allowing you to walk from one end to the other in 15 minutes.

Kadriorg

We walked from the ferry terminal through Kadriorg. The houses here are all wooden villas set deep in leafy plots. The horizontal timber cladding, deep eaves, exposed rafters, and tall, narrow windows are typical of late-19th-century Baltic timber houses. They all have steep red clay tile roofs with dormers, decorative wooden porches, and carved gables.

Song festival auditorium

We passed the open-air auditorium of the Estonian Song Festival. This is a large choral event, held every five years in July on the Tallinn Song Festival Grounds (Lauluväljak) simultaneously with the Estonian Dance Festival. The joint choir comprises more than 30,000 singers performing to an audience of 80,000. The iconic, arched stage was designed by Alar Kotli and completed in 1960. The hyperbolic-paraboloid arch was a significant engineering and architectural feat, creating excellent natural acoustics for large choirs and audiences and is considered a masterpiece of Soviet-era Finnish architecture.

Kadriorg, wooden house district Tallinn

Song festival auditorium, designed by Alar Kotli 1960

Lossi Plats

We climbed to a viewpoint in Toom Park, overlooking the city and contemplated the patchwork of neighbourhoods, coastline and many churches. The nearby Toompea Castle was an ancient Estonian stronghold in use since the 9th century AD.

The Alexander Nevsky Cathedral is an Eastern Orthodox cathedral built in 1894 when the country was part of the Russian Empire. It has eleven bells cast in Saint Petersburg, the largest of which weighs about 16 tons, and five onion domes, gilded-iron crosses. It is disliked by many Estonians as a symbol of former Russian oppression.

St. Mary's Cathedral is also located on Toompea Hill. The first church here was made of wood and here in 1219, when the Danes invaded Tallinn. In 1229, the Dominican friars arrived, replaced the old wooden church with stone.

Tallinn's Old Town is most renowned for its city wall and towers. The limestone protective wall was originally nearly four kilometres long, with eight gates and 46 towers. Today, about half of the wall and its towers still stand.

View of old town from Lossi Plat

St. Mary's Cathedral 1430

Alexander Nevsky Cathedral 1894

St. Mary's Cathedral

From here, we walked down Pikk Jalg, 'Long Leg,' the beautiful alley that connects the Lossi plats and the cathedral area to the lower town. This, and the adjacent Short Leg, were once the only way into the fortress and the route up to Toompea. The Long Leg was intended for the goods carts, horses and horsemen, while the Short Leg was pedestrian-only. The city wall next to the Long Leg was built in 1454–1455, and the current retaining wall opposite it was built in 1781.

All-linn – Lower Town

This area is one of the best preserved medieval towns in Europe and the authorities are continuing its rehabilitation. Major sights include Town Hall Square (Raekoja Plats), the city wall and towers, notably Kiek in de Kök, and several medieval churches.

St. Nicholas' Church (Niguliste) was originally built as a Catholic church in the 13th century by Westphalian merchants from Gotland. It turned Lutheran during the Protestant Reformation in the 1520s. Saint Nicholas was the only church in Tallinn which remained untouched by the iconoclasm of the Protestant Reformation. The head of the congregation poured

Kiek in de Kök and Maiden';s Tower on city wall 1475

Pikk Jalg, 'Long Leg, alley from upper to lower part of city

molten lead into the locks of the church, and the large, unruly mob could not break in.

The City Walls of Tallinn are the medieval defensive walls constructed around the city. The first wall was commissioned by Margaret Sambiria in 1265. Since then, the walls have been extended and strengthened. The walls and many gates remain largely intact today. The two round stone towers with red conical roofs ahead are the Kiek in de Kök and the Neitsitorn, the Maiden's Tower. The Kiek in de Kök was built as an artillery tower 1475. Cannonballs dating back to 1577 are still embedded in its outer walls.

The Raekoja plats, on the Town Hall Square, is a venue for festivals and concerts and the square also hosts a regular market. There has been a town hall in Tallinn since at least 1322. On the side of Town Hall, there is Raeapteek, the Town Hall Pharmacy, one of the oldest continuously running pharmacies in Europe, having been in business in the same house since the early 15th century. The surrounding buildings are 15th–19th-century guild and merchant houses.

Raekoja plats, Town Hall Square

Conclusion

The minimalism and simplicity of Scandinavian design was a major influence in renovating our home, Leveret Croft. We bought it in 1996, and the renovation took five years. We opened up the ground floor by taking down walls, and all the living rooms now have natural light from three sides. The walls are all clad with roll-bead boards. Only in the back room, which became our office, did we leave the boards natural. The rest of the house was painted. Timber takes paint quite differently from plaster. I decided to use eco-friendly paint from Farrow & Ball and Fired Earth, and bought a load of match pots. I painted these in 1-foot squares on the kitchen walls, and Scharlie and I independently scored combinations of two colours in both natural and artificial light. We then selected those colour combinations we both liked. These were all "knocked-back" umber tones that matched the colours in books on Scandinavian design I'd bought. I also made most of the furniture, including eight Hans Wegner-style beds.

The quality and craftsmanship of designs by Arne Jacobsen, Hans Wegner, and Aino and Alvar Aalto resonated with me and informed many of our furniture and lighting purchases. The Aaltos pioneered the use of bent plywood in the mid-1930s, and many of their pieces are still in production today. I bought one of their three-legged plywood stools at a junk shop in Cambridge in 1978, not knowing it was an Artek stool by Aalto.

choosing a colour scheme

	Kitchen	Dining	Living
gypsum		YY	Y
buttermilk		Y	
honey mist		?X	
cream	XX	XX	XX
oldwhite	X	X	Y
dutch white	X	X	Y
chalk white		X	
off white	X	X	
mineral grey	Y	Y	
palma grey	XX	X	
light blue		Y	
ballroom blue	X	Y	
powder blue		Y	
yellow drab	YY	Y	Y
hound lemon	Y	X	YY
sunflower yellow	Y	X	X
wild yellow	XX		
muffin	X	X	X
terre vert	XX	X	Y

Colours

Scroll through the colour palette or select your colour choice below.

Neutrals | Reds | Yellows | Greens | Blues | Darks

Churlish Green	Vert De Terre®	Pavilion Blue	Borrowed Light®
Saxon Green®	Lichen	Pale Powder	Skylight
Folly Green®	Chappell Green®	Teresa's Green®	Light Blue
Breakfast Room Green	Castle Gray®	Green Blue	Parma Gray
Calke Green®	Card Room Green®	Dix Blue®	Lulworth Blue®
Minster Green	Arsenic	Oval Room Blue®	Cook's Blue®

step 1 choose palette

Choosing colours for interior Leveret Croft

Match pot paint samples on kitchen wall

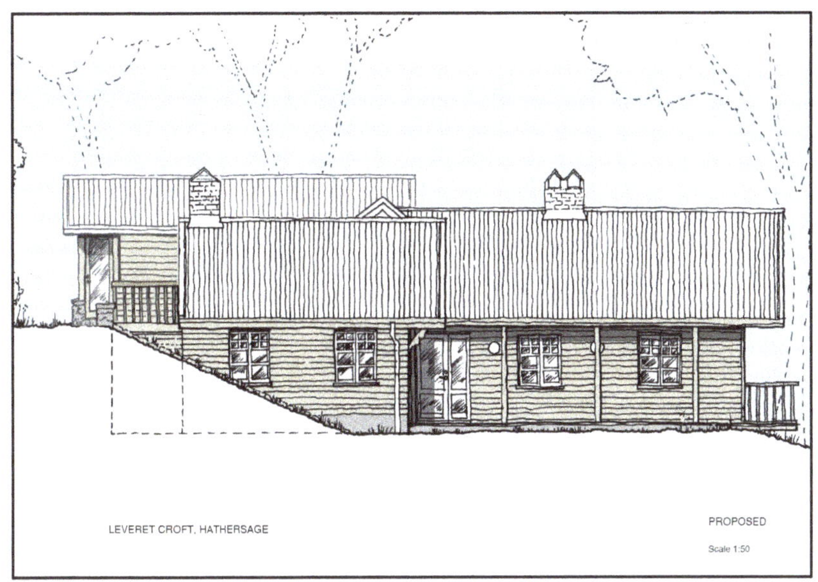

Extension, designed by Andrew de Carteret, Studio DC Architects 2013

Leveret Croft built 1900-1904

Finland

Land of lakes, midnight sun and saunas. Three-quarters of the country is forested, and there are nearly 200,000 lakes. Finland is consistently ranked as the world's happiest nation due to high living standards, equality, and work-life balance.

From the late 13th century, following the Northern Crusades, Finland became part of Sweden. In 1809, Finland was captured from Sweden and became an autonomous grand duchy within the Russian Empire. Following the Russian Revolution of 1917, Finland declared its independence. In the civil war, the following year, the anti-Communist Whites emerged victorious. Finland's status as a republic was confirmed in 1919.

During World War II, Finland fought against the Soviet Union in the Winter War and the Continuation War, and later against Nazi Germany in the Lapland War. As a result, it lost parts of its territory to the Soviet Union but retained its independence. During the Cold War, Finland maintained neutrality, and in 1995 it became a member of the European Union. Following the Russian invasion of Ukraine, Finland joined NATO in 2023.

View to Pielinen from Paha-Koli in Lieksa, Finland, 2019 Wikimedia Commons

In 1906 Finland became the first country in Europe to grant universal suffrage, and in the 1907 Finnish parliamentary election, Finland became the first country in the world to elect women to a national parliament.

Finland remained a largely rural and agrarian country until the 1950s, when it began rapid industrialisation and a Nordic-style welfare state, resulting in an advanced economy and high per capita income.

Replacing the old capital of Turku, Helsinki had become the economic and cultural centre of Finland by the mid-19th century. With an exodus of rural workers to the urban factories, new housing was desperately needed for both the affluent middle classes and the working classes. Housing for the wealthy was built around Kasarmitor Square, while Kallio was a working-class area. The traditional wooden houses were swept aside by a new type of accommodation, apartment blocks rising five or six storeys. These large apartment blocks were largely built by housing associations and housing companies, spurred on by State loans.

This urbanisation offered many opportunities for 'home-grown' architects and master builders who were aware of international trends, especially Arts and Crafts and Art Nouveau. Russification began in earnest under Czar

Nicholas II. resulting in demands for independence from Russia. Architects responded by incorporating Finnish motifs of pines, acorns, and fauna, notably bears.

In the 1920s, Finnish architecture transitioned from Nordic Classicism's restrained, geometric forms to Functionalism, championed by Alvar Aalto and others, who sought a humane, nature-inspired modernism. Their architecture was notable for its simplicity and originality, making a lasting impression on modern architecture.

.Paimio Sanatorium, designed by Alvar Aalto 1933. Photo Fabrice Foullet

www.ingramcontent.com/pod-product-compliance
Lightning Source LLC
LaVergne TN
LVHW052348100826
845147LV00012B/788
9781912460342